Lives and Times

Ray Kroc

M. C. Hall

Heinemann Library
Chicago, Illinois

© 2003 Heinemann Library
a division of Reed Elsevier Inc.
Chicago, Illinois

Customer Service 888-454-2279

Visit our website at www.heinemannlibrary.com

Designed by Herman Adler Design.
Illustrations by Robert Lawson
Printed and bound by Lake Book Manufacturing, Inc.

07 06 05 04 03
10 9 8 7 6 5 4 3 2 1

Library of Congress Cataloging-in-Publication Data
Hall, Margaret, 1947-
  Ray Kroc / M.C. Hall.
    v. cm. -- (Lives and times)
Includes bibliographical references and index.
Contents: Eating at restaurants -- The early years -- Growing up -- Becoming a salesperson -- The McDonald brothers -- A big idea -- A new company -- McDonald's grows -- New ideas -- Helping others -- Reaching out -- A baseball dream -- Learning more about Ray Kroc.
  ISBN 1-4034-3251-1 (lib. bdg.) -- ISBN 1-4034-4258-4 (pbk.)

  1. Kroc, Ray, 1902---Juvenile literature. 2. Restaurateurs--United States--Biography--Juvenile literature. 3. McDonald's Corporation--Juvenile literature. [1. Kroc, Ray, 1902- 2. Restaurateurs. 3. McDonalds Corporation.] I. Title. II. Lives and times (Des Plaines, Ill.)
  TX910.5.K76K76 2003
  338.7'616479573'092--dc21

                                        2003001523

Acknowledgments
The author and publishers are grateful to the following for permission to reproduce copyright material: p. 4 Mario Tama/Getty Images; pp. 5, 26 Bettmann/Corbis; pp. 6, 8, 11, 13, 14, 16, 17, 18, 20, 21, 22, 24, 27 McDonald's Corporation; p. 15 Sandy Felsenthal/Corbis; p. 19 Mark Peterson/Corbis SABA; p. 23 AP Wide World Photos; p. 25 Janet L. Moran/Oijoy photography; p. 28 Firdia Lisnawati/AP Wide World Photos; p. 29 Tim Boyle/Newsmakers/Getty Images

Cover photographs by Brian Warling/Heinemann Library, James Leynse/Corbis SABA, McDonald's Corporation.

Photo research by Dawn Friedman.

Special thanks to Michelle Rimsa for her comments in the preparation of this book.

Every effort has been made to contact copyright holders of any material reproduced in this book. Any omissions will be rectified in subsequent printings if notice is given to the publisher.

Some words are shown in bold, **like this.** You can find out what they mean by looking in the glossary.

Contents

Eating at Restaurants 4

The Early Years 6

Growing Up .8

Becoming a Salesperson 10

The McDonald Brothers 12

A Big Idea .14

A New Company 16

McDonald's Grows 18

New Ideas .20

Helping Others 22

Reaching Out 24

A Baseball Dream 26

Learning More About Ray Kroc 28

Fact File 30

Timeline 30

Glossary 31

More Books to Read 31

Index 32

Eating at Restaurants

All around the world, people like to eat at restaurants. Different kinds of restaurants serve different kinds of food.

Some restaurants serve fancy meals that can cost a lot of money.

Ray Kroc is shown here in front of one of his early restaurants.

Fast food restaurants serve meals quickly. The food does not cost as much as it would at a fancy restaurant. Ray Kroc helped to make fast food popular when he started the McDonald's restaurant **chain.**

The Early Years

Ray is shown here with his mother and sister.

Ray Kroc was born in Oak Park, Illinois, in 1902. As a boy, he loved baseball and playing the piano. Ray's mother was a piano teacher and she gave him lessons.

Ray also liked to work. As a little boy, he sold lemonade to make money. When he got older, he worked at a grocery store and a drugstore. Ray and some friends even started their own music store.

Even as a boy, Ray liked selling things to people.

Growing Up

When Ray was fifteen, the United States was fighting in **World War I.** Ray lied about his age so he could train to be an **ambulance** driver. He wanted to be able to help people who got hurt.

By the time Ray finished his training, the war was over.

Ray went back to high school, but he quit before he finished. Then he got a job selling ribbons. He also earned extra money by playing the piano at night.

Ray traveled from place to place to sell ribbons.

Becoming a Salesperson

In 1922, Ray started a new job selling paper cups to restaurants. Ray worked hard and became one of the company's best **salespeople.**

Restaurants bought paper cups for serving drinks.

The Multimixer made it easier to make milk shakes.

One of Ray's **customers** invented a machine called the Multimixer. It made five milk shakes at once. Ray thought the Multimixer was wonderful. In 1939, he started his own business selling the machine.

The McDonald Brothers

Ray traveled around the country selling Multimixers. Many of his **customers** in Southern California talked about a restaurant called McDonald's.

Mac and Dick McDonald used eight Multimixers in their restaurant.

Ray wanted to find out why Mac and Dave McDonald needed so many Multimixers. He parked outside their restaurant and watched. Many people lined up to buy hamburgers and milk shakes.

The original McDonald's had very few things on the menu.

A Big Idea

McDonald's
Speedee Service
MENU

HAMBURGERS	15¢
CHEESEBURGERS	19¢
MALT SHAKES	20¢
FRENCH FRIES	10¢
ORANGE	10¢
ROOT BEER	10¢
COFFEE	10¢
COKE	10¢
	10¢

A small menu helped McDonald's make food quickly and cheaply.

Ray talked to Mac and Dick. He thought they should start a **chain** of restaurants. However, the brothers did not want a lot of restaurants. They agreed to let Ray start the chain.

Ray and the McDonald brothers signed a **contract.** Mac and Dick would show Ray how they ran their restaurant. Ray would open McDonald's restaurants. Then he would give the brothers part of the money he made.

Every McDonald's restaurant was to have golden **arches.**

A New Company

In 1954, Ray opened his first McDonald's restaurant. He hoped to have many more restaurants, but he knew he could not do it alone. He started a company that sold **franchises** to other people.

Ray's first restaurant was in Des Plaines, Illinois.

Anyone who bought a franchise could open a McDonald's. Ray's company would help the owners set up their restaurants. By 1957, there were 38 McDonald's restaurants in the United States.

Ray and his partner planned new restaurants.

McDonald's Grows

Ray worked hard to make his company grow. He expected the people he hired to work hard, too. Ray thought that company leaders should know how to do every job their workers did.

Ray helped keep his restaurants clean. In this photo, he is hosing down a sidewalk.

Hamburger University teaches a group of new students about the restaurant business.

Ray wanted all McDonald's restaurant owners to be successful. He started a school called Hamburger University. Owners and **managers** went there to learn how to run a **fast food** restaurant.

New Ideas

Ray looked for ideas to make his company grow. Saving time by using hamburger buns that were already sliced was one idea. Having a clown named Ronald McDonald was another.

Ray added new foods to the menu. But McDonald's was best known for its hamburgers.

Another new idea was to have McDonald's restaurants outside of the United States. In 1967, restaurants opened in Canada and Puerto Rico. Almost every year after that, a McDonald's opened somewhere else in the world.

Ray was there when the first McDonald's was opened in Munich, Germany.

Helping Others

Ray gave money to people who wanted to help others.

Ray started the Kroc **Foundation** to raise money to fight **diseases.** In 1972, he celebrated his birthday by giving millions of dollars to hospitals, churches, libraries, **museums,** and other places.

Ray also helped others by giving them a chance to work for his company. In 1972, he received a special award for the opportunities he gave to so many young people.

Ray is at the left, getting the Horatio Alger Award.

Reaching Out

Ray wanted McDonald's workers to help people, too. In Philadelphia, McDonald's restaurant owners worked with football players to improve the community. In 1974, they started a house for families of sick children.

The families of sick children could stay at the Ronald McDonald House for free.

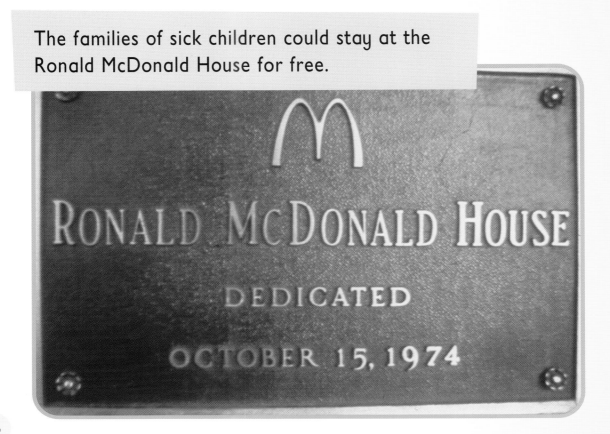

RONALD MCDONALD HOUSE
DEDICATED
OCTOBER 15, 1974

The Ronald McDonald House in Indianapolis opened in 1982.

Ray's company decided to teach people how to set up new Ronald McDonald Houses in their communities. For Ray's 75th birthday, friends started a **fund** to help build Ronald McDonald Houses all over the country.

A Baseball Dream

In 1974, Ray heard that the San Diego Padres baseball team was for sale. People were afraid the team would be sold to another city. Ray decided to buy it.

Ray and his wife liked to go to Padres games.

In 1984, the Padres made it to the World Series. Ray did not see the games. He had died earlier in the season. All of the players wore patches with Ray's initials.

Ray had been very proud of the Padres. They remembered him when they played.

Learning More About Ray Kroc

McDonald's is popular all over the world.
This restaurant is in Indonesia.

Ray Kroc reached his dream of running a **chain** of restaurants. By 2003, there were about 30,000 McDonald's restaurants in 121 countries around the world.

Ray's first restaurant in Des Plaines is now a **museum.** People can visit it to learn about Ray and the company he started. The McDonald brothers' restaurant in San Bernardino, California, is also a museum.

Museum displays show what the restaurants looked like when they first opened.

Fact File

- When Ray Kroc started McDonald's, he had trouble making French fries. He worked for three months to get them right.
- Ray Kroc's goal was to sell a hamburger, milk shake, and fries to a **customer** in less than one minute.
- "Quality, Service, and Cleanliness" became the McDonald's company motto in 1957.
- Ray Kroc became a member of the Advertising Hall of Fame in 1988.

Timeline

1902	Ray Kroc is born in Oak Park, Illinois
1922	Ray begins selling paper cups
1938	Ray begins selling Multimixers
1955	Ray opens his first McDonald's restaurant in Des Plaines, Illinois
1961	Hamburger University opens
1967	First McDonald's restaurants open outside the United States
1972	Ray gives away $7.5 million to help others
1974	Ray buys the San Diego Padres baseball team; first Ronald McDonald House opens in Philadelphia
1984	Ray Kroc dies

Glossary

ambulance vehicle used to carry people to a doctor or hospital

arch something with a curved shape

chain group of businesses with the same name and product

contract business agreement

customer someone who buys a product or service

disease sickness

fast food food that is served quickly and does not cost a lot

foundation group set up to raise and give away money to help others

franchise right to sell a company's products and use its name

fund source of money

manager person who is in charge of a group of workers

museum place where pieces of art or important parts of history are kept

salespeople people who sell things to others

World War I serious fight from 1914 to 1918 that involved European countries and the United States

More Books to Read

Hughes, Sarah. *My Uncle Owns a Deli.* Danbury, Conn.: Children's Press, 2001.

Schaefer, Lola. *Fast Food Restaurant.* Chicago: Heinemann, 2001.

An older reader can help you with this book:
Aaseng, Nathan. *Business Builders in Fast Food.* Oliver Press, 2001.

Index

Canada 21

Des Plaines, Illinois 16, 29, 30

fast food 5, 19
first McDonald's restaurant 16, 29
franchises 16, 17

Hamburger University 19, 30
hamburgers 13, 30

Kroc Foundation 22

McDonald, Mac and Dave 13
McDonald's restaurant 5, 15, 16, 17, 19, 21, 24, 28, 30
milk shakes 11, 13, 30
Multimixer 11, 12, 13, 30
museum 22, 29

piano 6, 9
Puerto Rico 21

restaurant chain 4, 14, 28
restaurants 4, 5, 10, 12, 13, 14, 15, 16, 17, 18, 19, 21, 24, 28, 29
Ronald McDonald House 24, 25
Ronald McDonald 20

San Diego Padres 26, 27, 30
selling 7, 9, 10, 12

workers 18, 24
World War I 8